ISLINGTON LIBRARIES

3 0120 00766258 8

GW00706109

l
Ho
ba
Ite

29

05

SUCCESSFUL TENNIS

David Lloyd

Illustrations by David Gifford

SACKVILLE BOOKS

ISLINGTON LIBRARIES

LIBRARY & ACC. No.	F
CLASS No.	796.342
CATG'D.	DATE

First published in 1989
by Sackville Books Ltd
Stradbroke, Suffolk, England

Text © David Lloyd
© Sackville Books Limited 1989

Designed and produced by Sackville Design Group Limited
Art Editor: Rolando Ugolini
Editor: Nick Bevan

British Library Cataloguing in Publication Data
Lloyd, David, 1948-
Successful tennis. — (Sackville sports clinic)
1. Lawn tennis
I. Title
796.342

ISBN 0 948615 24 9

All rights reserved. No part of this publication may be reproduced, stored in a
retrieval system, or transmitted, in any form or by any means, electronic,
mechanical, photocopying, recording or otherwise, without the prior
permission of the publishers.

Typeset by BPCC Printec Ltd, Diss, Norfolk, England

Reproduction by BPCC Bury Studio, Bury St Edmunds, Suffolk, England

Printed and bound by Serif Cowells plc, Ipswich, Suffolk.

Contents

David Lloyd was ranked in Britain's top ten tennis players for ten years, and highlights of his career include wins over Ilie Nastase, Jimmy Connors, Jan Kodes and Brian Gottfried, and a win in the doubles semi-final at Wimbledon. He was an established member of the British Team and has coached the British Wightman Cup Team for several years. Now he comments on tennis on television and runs a series of indoor tennis clubs with teams of experienced coaches. The David Lloyd Clubs enjoy an unparalleled reputation in this field.

Introduction Islington Libraries

When I was a kid, you couldn't keep me off the football pitch — I played all the time. All I wanted was to be a footballer.

Thirty or more years on, I play as much golf as I can. It's a game which fascinates me.

However, when it comes to competitive sport, neither football nor golf, nor, as far as I'm concerned, any game, compares with tennis. For me, tennis is simply the greatest sport there is.

Why is it so great? For many reasons — but there are two major ones. Firstly, no matter what your standard, you can always enjoy a game of tennis, virtually anywhere in the world — but the second, and more powerful reason is that, to be a good tennis-player you need a bit of everything in your make-up.

Footballers, rugby players, athletes — they can all get to the top on strength, speed, fitness, and aggression with limited physical skills. On the other hand, golfers, cricketers and the like need highly developed skills and techniques — but they don't have to be great athletes. And then there is tennis — and to get anywhere near the top in tennis you need a combination of skill, flair, technique, speed, strength and aggression. I can't think of any sport which makes such demands on a player.

These days, tennis-players cannot get by on skill alone. The top men have realised this over the last ten years, and the ladies are rapidly catching up. Now they have to be athletes as well as racket players.

Tennis has changed enormously since I first started. Changes in the construction of rackets mean that the ball is hit 30% harder than it was twenty years ago.

That progress has been matched in the development of the game, all over the world. The average club player can now go almost anywhere in the world and find a club where they can play — and the facilities will be top-class.

More and more top-quality indoor centres are springing up, making tennis a game which can be played all the year round in pleasant surroundings and comfortable conditions.

Hopefully, these improving facilities will attract more players to the sport. The more people who play the game, the higher the standard will become at the top.

CHAPTER ONE

Playing by the book

I honestly believe that there are a lot of people who have been discouraged from playing tennis because they could not produce the style of shots which their coaches demanded, or which the coaching manual recommended.

To those frustrated players, I aim part of this book — I'm not interested in style, to me it's irrelevant. The important question to ask is, 'Does it work?' If you can get the ball over the net using a frying pan or a fishing net, that's great by me. How you hold the racket and how you swing doesn't matter — as long as the end result is right.

I'm not going to blind you with science — too many coaching books I've read do that. If you go to Wimbledon or any great tournament, and watch the world's top players, you will soon realize that every individual has his own style. Two hundred players — two hundred different shots. After a while you could identify the players from the way they swing their rackets — style really is irrelevant to them, so it shouldn't matter to you either!

What you may not notice is that every one of those top players does the same thing at the vital time — the split second before and after making contact with the ball — what we call 'the hitting zone'. That brief moment is what really counts — and you have to get it right.

You can scrap the coaching manuals of the past — Bjorn Borg, John McEnroe, Jimmy Connors and Chris Evert have seen to that. They broke all the old rules and went on to become outstanding champions.

What they did was to improvize their own styles — but they still observed the vital principles at the critical points in the swing.

Bjorn Borg changed the entire game almost single-handed. He destroyed all the old theories about what is the right way to hold a racket. He built his entire game around a totally unorthodox, exaggerated forehand grip, so producing a style which was to win him six French Open and five Wimbledon titles. His forehand grip was so far round the handle that he was forced to use two hands to make a backhand shot — the grip change would have been too big for him to manage an orthodox backhand.

Now a new generation of Swedish players has grown up in

the Borg style. It works! You have only to look at the number of Swedes in the rankings. It was Borg who more or less invented the modern game of heavy top-spin ground-strokes — it may be boring — but it's effective.

With the assistance of modern racket-design and using enormous top-spin, players these days hit the ball 30% harder than they did twenty years ago. Today's game is based on power.

Racket style

When I first started, rackets were made of wood — and they were all the same size. Now you can't give away a wooden racket — the modern materials are graphite, ceramics or boron. Equipment has made the jump into the space-age.

Today's rackets are lighter and stronger — designed to go through the air faster, and this allows today's players to develop more pace on the ball and more spin. Racket-heads are bigger too — up to 42% bigger than old models — and this gives more power and control.

Although the modern game could justifiably be said to be more boring, due to the long, top-spin, base-line rallies, the development of the racket has created a whole new range of shots. A skilful player can whip the racket through the ball to produce top-spin lobs — or can flick a passing shot or half-volley when they are under pressure. In fact, contrary to the supposition that the new, high-tech racket has made the game more boring, it has opened up the variety of the game, giving more scope for the adventurous and skilled player.

In this book I hope there is something for every standard, from the beginner to the advanced player. I know I have already said that style is unimportant on most shots — but that doesn't mean to say that the unorthodox approach is a sound one for everybody. I have therefore set out a basic, solid technique for each stroke — one which should suit most players. The point which I emphasize is that of the importance of observing the key elements in each shot. After that, it's up to every player to improvize his own style around the basic swing.

In golfing circles they say, 'Drive for show — putt for dough'. It's just the same in tennis — it's not the style that matters, what is important is to win the point. Winning has always been important to me — I hope I can help you to be a winner too.

The equipment

Nobody can tell you what size or type of racket will be right for you. That's not how it works. As an illustration, the great Australian, Ken Rosewall, used a racket with a five-inch grip. He was not much over five feet tall and had small hands — yet he chose a massive five-inch grip. In complete contrast Boris Becker, who is massive, uses a very light racket with a four-and-a-half-inch grip size. (I know, he gave one of his rackets to my son, Scott, who could play with it easily at the age of 12!)

This just goes to show that you can't lay down rules. The only thing you can go by is what feels right to you. Beware, though — what feels right in the shop may not feel so good when you start hitting real balls on the court. My advice is to go to a sports shop which has test rackets available so that you can try them out. Never buy a racket without hitting some shots with it.

In general, rackets are a lot lighter than they used to be — and the variety of racket-head sizes gives you a lot more choice. You may find the wide range which is available rather bewildering. If you do, try asking the advice of a professional coach if possible.

If you are just beginning, you don't need to spend a fortune on a racket. Since you are not looking for a high-performance model, something in the £30-40 price range is perfectly good. I would recommend the 'big head' size — and that applies to young children too. The reason is that big-head rackets give you the advantage of bringing the hitting area nearer the hand.

In Czechslovakia they actually teach children to hit the ball with their hand first, before letting them start with a racket — and as you've probably noticed, the Czechs don't do too badly when it comes to producing good players!

For the older player too, whose eyesight and reactions are not as sharp as they once were, these big 'maxi' rackets are a tremendous advantage. Indeed, they have revolutionized the game for veterans — and volleys are twice as easy with a big racket.

A more advanced player will probably find the mid-size racket most suitable — it gives slightly more control without loss of power. As a rule, the better player you are, the more you expect from your racket — and the more you will have to pay.

But whatever your standard, it's still a matter of choice, feel and personal taste. How does the racket feel in your hand? How does it swing? How does it suit your groundstokes? Can you serve with it?

Modern rackets, made from graphite fibres or similar materials, are much stiffer than the old wooden-framed ones. There is no 'give' in the racket — and this can lead to tennis elbow for some people. It can often help to attach one of the many anti-vibration devices now available to the strings. These absorb the shock waves before they can travel up the racket handle into your arm.

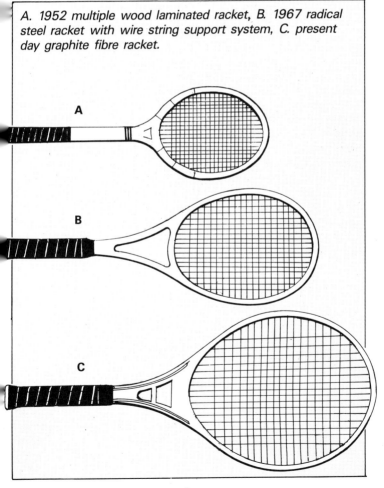

A. 1952 multiple wood laminated racket, B. 1967 radical steel racket with wire string support system, C. present day graphite fibre racket.

A

B

C

CHAPTER TWO

The groundstrokes

Groundstrokes ARE tennis — the meat of the game. Look on them as the main course, with the service as the starter and the volleys as the dessert.

Solid, dependable groundstrokes are essential if you want to play tennis at a good standard. The best service in the world will ultimately never be able to disguise — or make up for — a lack of ability off the ground.

I have one overall piece of advice which applies equally to groundstrokes and volleys. Never let the ball dominate you — you must dominate the ball. By that I mean that you should never let the ball come to you. You must go to meet the ball — you must be positive. If you allow the ball to come to you, it means you are on the defensive and your shot will be late and lack power. Remember, you can only win by attacking the ball.

There are three key elements in good 'groundies':

- Early preparation
- Transfer of weight from back foot to front foot
- Follow through

Early preparation is a must — get the racket-head back in plenty of time for the shot. Coaches in America emphasize this above all else. It's the first thing they teach, so when they get a youngster on court, they feed him a ball and shout, 'racket back' as they release the ball. The kid will almost certainly become heartily fed-up with those two words, 'racket back', but he will quickly learn to prepare early for the stroke.

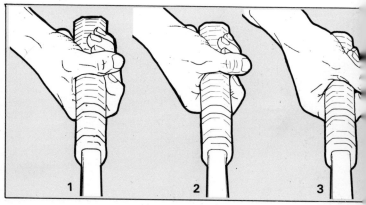

Early preparation puts you in control of the shot and gives you the chance to develop a rhythm without rushing. Most importantly, it allows you to step into the shot and meet the ball early — and this automatically leads to the correct transfer of weight.

Your body weight must shift on to the front foot as the forward swing brings the racket into the hitting area. After contact, the follow-through should take the racket along the line of the ball, so that the swing finishes at head-height.

These basic principles are vital, no matter what your grip or the shape of your swing. They have nothing to do with style — and they apply to both backhand and forehand drives. Get the three stages right, and you are well on the way to a successful groundstroke.

The Grips

1 *The Bjorn Borg forehand grip. Note how far round the handle the hand is, enabling him to hit naturally with top-spin.*

2 *The Western forehand grip used by players such as Ivan Lendl and Boris Becker. It's not as extreme as Borg's but the palm of the hand is right behind the ball.*

3 *The Eastern forehand grip, favoured by the classical strikers such as John Newcombe.*

4 *The continental forehand or backhand grip. This grip is used on the forehand by Steffi Graf — although her thumb would be wrapped round the front plane instead of up the handle as shown.*

5 *The Eastern backhand grip used by most of the great backhand strikers.*

6 *Exaggerated continental backhand used by a few players who hit heavy top-spin on the backhand.*

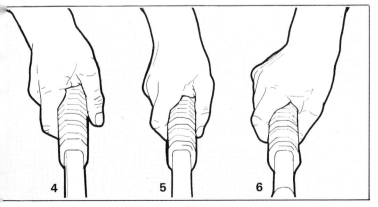

CHAPTER THREE

The forehand drive

These days anything (well, almost anything) goes on the forehand — as long as it works.

The old textbooks insisted on a classical 'shake-hands' type of grip, on a sideways-on stance, on a big, looped swing, and on the racket-head staying above the wrist. So if you aren't in pursuit of a classic style, it's not necessary. Of course it works — but then so do other styles.

Some of the most fearsome forehands in world tennis today are struck with the grip right on top of the handle (as you would hold a frying pan), with an open stance (facing the net), and with a dropped wrist. Boris Becker, and Ivan Lendl hit their forehands this way — they are great forehands which break all the old rules — but they still follow the basic principles I have described before. They give themselves plenty of time for the shot, they step into it, and finish with a long follow-through.

Becker and Lendl, like Bjorn Borg, have a very high take-back of the racket, with a very big loop in the swing to bring the racket-head down under the ball so that they hit 'on the up'. On the other hand, many leading players take the racket straight back on a low swing, and just bring it straight back up on the forward swing from low to high. Their style works just as well for them — they are still observing the basic rules.

That's why I say that style doesn't matter. Just choose the method which works for you, and once you've found it, stick to it — and to the basic principles.

The same applies to the way you grip your racket —

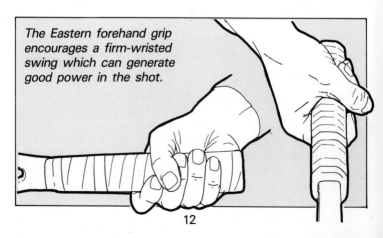

The Eastern forehand grip encourages a firm-wristed swing which can generate good power in the shot.

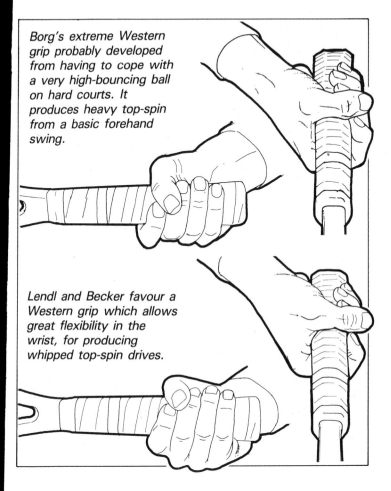

Borg's extreme Western grip probably developed from having to cope with a very high-bouncing ball on hard courts. It produces heavy top-spin from a basic forehand swing.

Lendl and Becker favour a Western grip which allows great flexibility in the wrist, for producing whipped top-spin drives.

whatever you find comfortable is right for you — provided you can hit good shots that way. It's only wrong if the shots don't work.

Borg's grip was the most unorthodox and exaggerated I've ever seen. At first glance you'd have said it was impossible for him to control the ball and generate power — but he could, and many players have copied him.

Personally, I wouldn't recommend such an extreme grip. For one thing, it has its restrictions. It's impossible to hit a forehand slice or 'chip' shot with that grip — and such a big grip-change is necessary to enable you to hit a one-handed backhand that it is almost inevitable that you have to make this stroke using two hands. However, this worked for Borg, and he got to be world champion — so you can't dismiss it entirely.

Becker and Lendl keep the palm of the hand on top of the racket handle (assuming the racket is lying flat). It's less extreme, and more comfortable for the average player, allowing you to hit with basic top-spin.

Steffi Graf's forehand is the single, most devastating shot in tennis today, either men's or women's — and she uses a classic forehand grip. To find it, hold the racket perpendicular with your free hand, then 'shake hands' with the handle, using your racket hand. The Graf forehand is magnificent. She prepares early and hits through the ball with tremendous power, finishing with a very high follow-through — in fact, she conforms exactly to all the vital requirements.

I'm a believer in every player developing his own style within the framework of those vital elements, but I can provide a basis for a technique which should generate solid, consistent strokes for most players.

Footwork and positioning

As with all shots in the game, footwork is important, not to say vital. Try to get into the habit of taking quick, short steps

s you prepare for your shots. The nearer you get to the point
of contact, the shorter your steps need to be. This will allow
you to make last-minute adjustments to your positioning.

Don't get into position too early. Time your movement so
that you can step into the shot as you swing. Stay on your
toes and never be flat-footed.

Correct transference of weight from the back to the front foot is vital in ground shots. As the racket begins the forward swing, the player shifts his weight forward on to the front foot. Note the contact point just in front of the leading hip and, below, the high follow-through.

THE FOREHAND DRIVE

In preparation for your forehand drive, turn your shoulders so that the left one (in right-handed players) points towards the ball. Take the racket back high, so that the forward swing completes a continuous loop, allowing the racket to come down and approach the ball from below. Judge your position so that you make contact with the hitting arm fully extended. Your aim should be to hit the ball when it is about level with, or just in front of the left hip.

In the hitting zone, keep your wrist firm and your head still with your eyes locked on to the ball. Then, after contact, your racket-head must follow through along the line of the ball's direction. Hit 'through' the ball, letting the racket-head follow the ball to finish on a high swing.

It is as important in tennis as it is in golf to keep your head still — don't lift your head on impact, but stay 'down' on the ball. In the hitting zone, the key point is to make sure you present the full face of the racket to the ball. Don't underestimate the importance of the follow-through — it is actually more critical than the backswing, as it dictates the direction of the ball.

As a check on your follow-through, look at the position of the bicep-muscle on your upper arm when you have completed your swing. If you've followed through correctly, the muscle will be nestling against your chin. If that muscle is not close up to your chin, you know you are not hitting through the ball correctly.

On page 14 the high take-back used by Becker, Lendl and others is shown, with the looped swing needed to bring the racket down to the hitting zone. The action below is the alternative. The racket is taken straight back on a low plane, and the forward swing traces the reverse arc back to the hitting zone.

Forehand drive — variations

The basic forehand swing produces a shot which can be hit flat or with slight top-spin — however, these days very few balls are hit flat in advanced play. Heavy top-spin is a basic requirement — it allows the ball to be hit harder but with a greater margin of safety, because the top-spin drags the ball down inside the court.

Top-spin

Hitting with top-spin requires little variation on the basic swing. Preparation and take-back are the same, but the loop in the forward swing is accentuated by dropping the wrist and allowing the racket to come up to make contact with the ball from a steeper angle. The lower the racket head drops, the more top-spin you can apply to the ball — the racket makes contact with the back of the ball in a brushing action, meeting the ball with the head in a vertical position. Fractionally after contact, the arm and wrist combine to turn the racket face slightly over the ball. As in the basic drive, the follow-through takes the racket-head through the line of the shot, ending at head height.

Top-spin forehand
To apply top-spin on the ball the racket comes up to meet the ball from below. The racket brushes up the back of the ball, and sweeps over it.

The key factor for hitting a top-spin forehand is to make
re that the racket-face is not 'closed' too early. The full face
the racket must make contact with the ball. If the racket
ce is turned over the ball too early, the ball will either end in
e net or will lack power and land short.

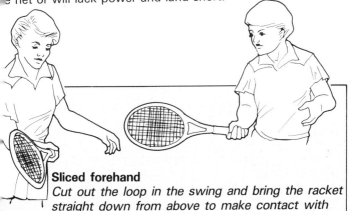

Sliced forehand
*Cut out the loop in the swing and bring the racket
straight down from above to make contact with
the back of the ball.*

he sliced forehand

his shot is more rarely used in men's tennis these days. That
partly due to the exaggerated forehand grips which many
layers use, making the sliced shot almost impossible to hit —
nd also because the slice causes the ball to 'float' in the air,
nd is therefore a defensive shot.

However, you can use the slice as a variation in a base-line
ally, or as an approach shot when the ball is short and can
e hit early, from above the height of the net.

Preparation for the shot is basically the same, with a
lightly higher take-back and an early shoulder-turn. The
orward swing cuts out the loop, the racket-face opens
lightly and comes straight down to the hitting point, making
ontact with the back of the ball. The follow-through takes
he racket-head down through the ball, before rising again to
he finish of the swing.

The underswing imparted to the ball will cause it to float
hrough the air, but on faster surfaces such as grass, it will
hoot, and keep low on bouncing, giving your opponent a
roblem in trying to dig out his return.

That is particularly useful when you are coming in to the
et behind a sliced approach shot. It makes it harder to pass
ou, and the slower trajectory of the slice gives you more
ime to close in to a good volleying position.

CHAPTER FOUR

The backhand drive

The backhand drive is a slightly more technical stroke than the forehand. There are fewer variations to the basic action that can work effectively.

On the other hand, the same principles that apply to the forehand are just as relevant for the backhand — precise footwork, early preparation and a good shoulder turn. The difference with these elements for the backhand is that the shoulder-turn is exaggerated. The great backhand strikers turn so far that their back is completely turned towards the net — it is not the shoulder, but the shoulder-blade which points at the ball.

A sideways-on position is also more important for backhand shots — only one player hits the ball on the backhand with an open stance, and that is Boris Becker. Don't try to copy Boris — he plays table-tennis shots on the tennis court and gets away with it, but that's only because he is phenomenally strong in the wrist and forearm.

Mere mortals, Ivan Lendl included, need to get the front

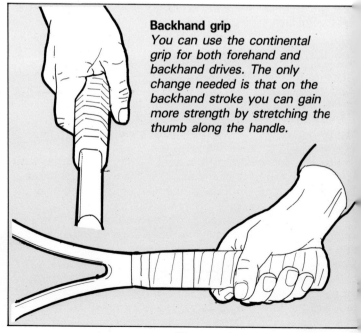

Backhand grip
You can use the continental grip for both forehand and backhand drives. The only change needed is that on the backhand stroke you can gain more strength by stretching the thumb along the handle.

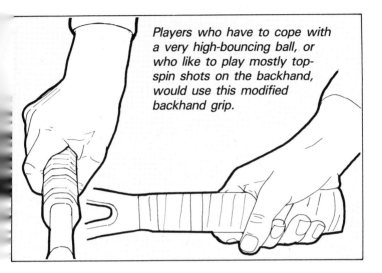

Players who have to cope with a very high-bouncing ball, or who like to play mostly top-spin shots on the backhand, would use this modified backhand grip.

foot well across to provide balance for the shot. Just as for the forehand, you should aim to time the movement so that you can step into the shot as you swing the racket.

As ever, early preparation is vital — in fact, if anything, it is even more necessary on the backhand, because the ideal contact point with the ball is slightly further forward than on the forehand side, well in front of the leading foot.

Even though you are using a single-handed backhand, it is still very important to use your free hand to support the racket-head on the backswing. Take the racket back high,

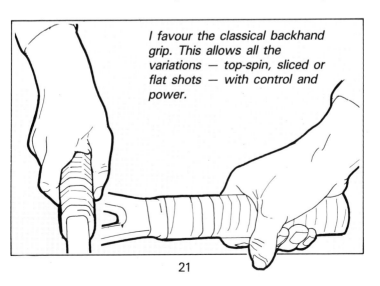

I favour the classical backhand grip. This allows all the variations — top-spin, sliced or flat shots — with control and power.

A good early preparation, with full shoulder-turn, is the key to a good backhand drive. The player, far left, has just started to unwind into the shot, as her weight comes forward. On the right, note how the free hand supports the racket-head.

with the non-hitting hand supporting the racket at the throat.

Start the forward swing with the same loop as for the forehand, bringing the racket down and forward to approach the hitting area at a level just below that of the ball. (Your free hand will have released the racket at the start of the downward swing — the better players subconsciously use their free hand as a counter-balance as their shoulders unwind into the shot).

As the racket swings into the hitting zone, you must keep your wrist locked firmly, with your head still and your eyes glued to the ball. When you make a single-handed stroke, your knee-bend must be very pronounced so that your hands

can go right down, keeping the racket-head from dropping too far below the wrist.

Of all the men players today, the best single-handed backhand is that of Stefan Edberg — he has a terrific shoulder-turn and superb balance. He just unwinds into the shot, giving his opponent very little clue as to the intended direction.

Amongst the ladies, take a look at Catarina Lindquist of Sweden — her personal beauty is exceeded only by that of her backhand, it's sheer perfection!

Backhand drive — the variations

Up until twenty years ago, only the most advanced players used a top-spin backhand. Many Wimbledon titles were won without the shot being used once. Nowadays, however, the top-spin backhand is an essential part of any player's game, even at club standard.

The top-spin backhand

The top-spin backhand is essentially an attacking shot. The top-spin allows you to hit the ball hard, high over the net with a good safety margin — and the resulting high bounce puts your opponent under pressure.

To put top spin on a backhand requires just the same variation to the basic technique as does a top-spin forehand — a deepening of the loop on the backswing to allow the racket-head to approach the hitting area from below. Also, particularly on a single-handed stroke, you must achieve a full

On the top-spin backhand, make sure the full face of the racket makes contact with the ball. The racket-face only closes over the ball fractionally after contact, thereby imparting the top-spin.

bend of the knees, so that you can get right down to the shot. This prevents the racket-head from dropping too low below the wrist.

The full face of the racket should make contact with the ball and, at impact, the racket-face should be vertical. Immediately after contact, you make a combined movement of the forearm and wrist to roll the racket over the ball. As with the top-spin forehand, if you do this too early, the ball will find the net or land short with loss of power.

Early preparation is vital, you simply cannot hit a top-spin backhand unless you make contact with the ball in front of the leading hip.

You can use top spin to whip the ball low over the net across court to seek out sharp angles — and this shot is also the best option to use when trying for a passing shot. The spin will make the ball dip sharply over the net, making it tough for the volleyer to hit a winning shot, even when in the correct position to play the ball.

The sliced backhand

The sliced backhand is still one of the basic shots of both men's and women's games at top level, even if not used as much as in the past. It is essentially a defensive shot — but properly executed at the right time, it can be deadly.

You can hit a sliced backhand with a much shorter backswing, so it is an ideal shot to use when you are under pressure, when you are forced wide out of the court, or if you have to dig out a very low ball.

Play the stroke with the same shoulder-turn and high take-back as for the basic stroke. Open the racket-face slightly and bring it straight down and forward to meet the ball from above, hitting down and through the ball, finishing with a high follow-through.

Note the long follow-through on the sliced backhand. The racket follows the line of the ball and the player's bodyweight is right behind the shot. Note how the racket-face opens slightly before contact.

The two-handed backhand

The tennis purists of the past spurned the use of double-handed shots, basically because of the limitations such shots impose when reaching for wide balls. However, the success over the last twenty years of players such as Bjorn Borg, Jimmy Connors, Chris Evert and many others has destroyed theories that two-handed backhands are more of a handicap than an asset.

Certainly for Jimmy and Chris the double-hander was the big gun in their armoury. Some handicap! Now, a whole generation of players has grown up using a two-handed backhand, so now it has become orthodox.

Today's players overcome the restrictions of the double-handed backhand by being more mobile, running faster and learning to cultivate a single-handed shot for those occasions when they are forced so wide that they can't play their normal stroke. On the plus side, they have the advantages of the two-handed shot — extra power, control and disguise.

The basic shape of the shot is similar to the single-handed

version — but instead of the free hand supporting the racket at the throat on the backswing, it drops down the handle to nestle tightly against the dominant hand.

You need to be even more precise on your footwork here than for the orthodox, single-handed shot, in order to cope with the shorter reach and the reduced freedom which the style allows. Your stance needs to be slightly more open, with the front foot further down the court and the shoulders well turned.

The looped swing is very much the same as for the single-handed stroke, and the extra strength of the second hand makes it easier to drop the racket-head to hit with top spin.

Good shoulder-turn is essential on the two-handed backhand. Positioning has to be precise because of the restricted reach. You need more leg action on the two-hander to get more power into the shot. Note the shorter follow-through than for the orthodox backhand.

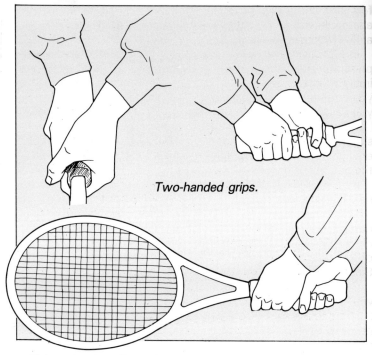

Two-handed grips.

This style also allows for a degree of disguise on the direction of the shot, as the supporting hand provides the strength to give yourself some different options — you can accelerate the racket-head into the ball at the last second, so as to make contact early for a cross-court shot, or alternatively, hold the racket-head back fractionally late to play down the line.

The style you use is down to personal choice. Try swinging a racket — you'll soon be able to feel which stroke is more comfortable, and gauge whether or not you could do with the extra power that a double-handed shot can generate. If you feel the double-handed shot is for you, that's fine — there's nothing wrong with that these days. For an ideal example of style, watch Chris Evert — and for sheer aggression and power, take a look at Jimmy Connors — he throws himself into the ball, both feet off the ground, really attacking it.

A grounding of ground strokes

So, those are the strokes — the meat of the game. Now you need to think about when to use them. The idea of the forehand and backhand drives is to create a solid and adaptable stroke. One that can be grooved into a repetitive action which will not break down under pressure.

In a base line rally, your ground shots must be deep to put pressure on your opponent and prevent him from taking the initiative in the rally. Depth is more efficient than speed — if you can hit your drives deep enough and for long enough, you will eventually force the short ball which you can attack.

When you play a baseline rally, forget about the net — it shouldn't come into play at all. You can hit the ball high enough, with a little top spin for control, not to worry about the net.

If your opponent is threatening you by coming in to the net, then clearly you must hit your groundshot lower. However, be careful not to make the mistake of going for an outright winner off the first ball. Use top spin for control, to dip the ball over the net, forcing the volleyer to play the ball off his toes. Make him hit up — work for an opening. Similarly, when you get the short ball, step in and attack it.

Stay on the balls of your feet and try to move to the ball with sideways steps, so you can face the net and stay in balance. Move to make your shot quickly and early — try never to play the stroke on the run. Get to the hitting point early so that you can check your momentum and compose yourself for the shot. Remember too, never to get impatient with rallies.

Just one final tip for groundshots. Always try to hit the outside of the ball — this is true of all the great groundstrokes in the game. It increases your control of the shot and the theory applies whether you are hitting with top spin or slice.

Hitting round the ball means you are dominating it. Once you get inside the ball, your wrist has come through ahead of the racket and the ball is at the mercy of the elements — it isn't hit, it's drifting. Having said that, two great players — Jimmy Connors and Chris Evert — both hit their forehands on the inside of the ball. They still hit great shots, but if they have a slight weakness, it's on the low forehand where they have come inside the ball.

Steffi Graf is a perfect exponent of hitting round the outside of the ball. She almost hooks her forehand and that gives her control to wallop the ball.

CHAPTER FIVE

The volley

In the previous chapter I described the groundshots as the main course of the game and the volleys as the dessert.

So, to continue in the same vein, I suppose you could say I have a sweet tooth for tennis. I just love hitting volleys. For me there's no greater satisfaction in the game than that of punching away a winning volley.

I could happily play tennis without ever hitting a groundshot — volleying is such fun. It's an aggressive shot — a winning shot.

The best way I can describe the action of the volley is to say that it's like picking apples off a tree. Imagine you are standing in front of a tree loaded with fruit — you just stretch out your hand and take one.

That is basically all you do when you hit a volley. You never swing the racket, you just go forward to meet the ball. There is no backswing — you don't need it and there's no time for it. You just generate speed on your volley by using the pace of the ball coming at you.

The volley is the only shot in the game where you must grip the racket tightly. On groundstrokes and on the serve you can use a relaxed grip — but not on the volley. It has to be tight. Lock your wrist firmly as you play the shot, so that your arm and racket are one unit and move as one towards the ball.

Never drop the racket-head when you play a volley — even when playing a shot off your toes. The racket-head must always stay above the wrist.

Volley technique

There is not much room for flexibility in volley technique. There are certain principles you must observe, and there is not a lot of scope for you to improvize. For example, there is no backswing, and the follow-through is short and sharp. The volley is a punch rather than a stroke.

You are also a bit limited on the type of grip you can use. You need a 'chopper' grip, a notch or two further round the handle in an anti-clockwise direction from the 'shake-hands' or 'Eastern' forehand grip.

When someone hits the ball hard at you at the net, you may not have time to move your feet — but you must pivot with your shoulders to give yourself enough room to push forward.

The volley is purely a forward movement — perhaps a good way of describing the shot is to call it a 'jab', like a boxer's leading punch. Ideally you should step forward into the shot, so your whole body goes to meet the ball, the racket extending in front. Sometimes you have no time for that, so you must just lock your wrist, pivot your shoulders and push the racket forwards. You must make contact with the full face of the racket and hit right through the back of the ball.

The forehand volley

When you have the time to do so, prepare for a forehand volley by turning your shoulders and stepping across with your left foot (for right-handed players). Keep the racket-head high, then punch it down and forward to make contact with the ball in front. Remember, the grip must be tight and your wrist locked firm.

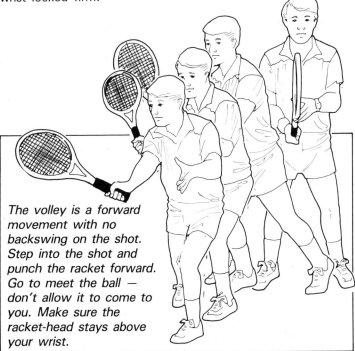

The volley is a forward movement with no backswing on the shot. Step into the shot and punch the racket forward. Go to meet the ball — don't allow it to come to you. Make sure the racket-head stays above your wrist.

Get your weight going forward behind the ball as you hit the volley. Really bend those knees and keep your body flexible when you have to play a low volley. You must get right down, to keep the racket-head above the wrist.

On a low forehand volley, you must make a full knee-bend, so that your knuckles on the racket hand are almost on the ground as you meet the ball. Don't let the racket-head drop below the wrist.

With a low volley, turn the racket-face under the ball on impact to give it some back spin — it provides control. If you are hitting the ball from below the height of the net, you have to hit up, so the under spin helps lift the ball off the strings.

The hardest thing for players to understand about the volley is the 'no swing' rule. I find a sure-fire way to cure players who swing at their volleys is to make them stand up against a wall — then I hit balls for them to volley. If their racket hits the wall, it means they have taken a swing at the ball. They soon learn to come forward and punch the shot.

The backhand volley

Exactly the same principles apply to the backhand volley as do to the forehand of the shot. To prepare, you pull your left shoulder back (if you are right-handed), and step forward and cross with your right foot.

Turn the shoulders and punch the racket away from your body. As on the ground shots, transfer the weight from the back foot as you step into the shot and follow through along the line of the shot.

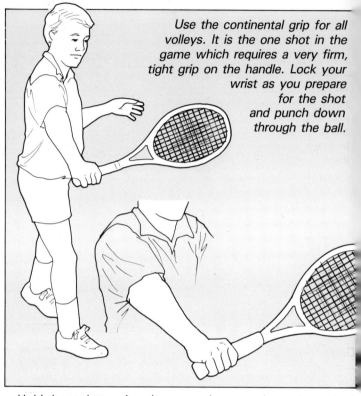

Use the continental grip for all volleys. It is the one shot in the game which requires a very firm, tight grip on the handle. Lock your wrist as you prepare for the shot and punch down through the ball.

Hold the racket, using the same chopper grip, and punch the racket head away from your body as your weight goes forward on to the front foot. Think of it as 'leaning' on the ball with your shoulder. Keep the follow-through short and crisp, taking the racket-head down through the back of the ball.

Once again, as for the forehand volley, on the low shot you must turn the racket-face under the ball on contact to get under spin for lift and control. Often you may need to hit the low volley across court to give the ball time to clear the net. To get the angle right, the racket must meet the ball right out in front so that you have the freedom to take the racket-face around the ball. Make sure you get right down to the shot, so that you can keep the racket-head above the wrist.

Backhand volleys can be a problem for double-handed players — it is possible to volley effectively with two hands, but the technique is difficult. Therefore I think it's wise to encourage young players to develop a one-handed volley at an early stage.

To help control your volleys, use your free hand to assist your balance as you step into the shot.

Volley summary

Don't be afraid of the ball — never go back to take a volley — you need to be positive and aggressive. When you have got up to the net, you are in the driving seat as far as the rally is concerned.

Stay on the balls of your feet, so you are poised to react fast. The ball is going to come at you twice as fast when you are at the net, so be prepared for it.

The 'ready' position is one with your racket held well out in front, its head well up. Be ready to turn your shoulders and step into the shot — always going forward, *into* it. Don't wait for it to come to you.

Watch Pat Cash on the volley — he's probably the best volleyer in the world today, and is terrific entertainment. His low volleys are classical — he gets right down and punches the ball away with great pace.

Martina Navratilova has a magnificient backhand volley. Her racket goes right out in front of her to meet the ball. Left-handers generally tend to have good backhand volleys because they get to hit thousands of balls that way when they play right-handers.

Remember, the margin for error increases dramatically if you start to swing at a volley — so don't. Just *block* the ball.

CHAPTER SIX

The service and smash

The serve is a unique shot in tennis, and one to which an enormous amount of mystique is attached. There are three points which, in theory, should make it the easiest one to master.

Firstly, it's the only stroke which is totally in your control as the striker. Secondly, you get two chances. In every shot in the game you are governed to some extent by your opponent. The stroke you play depends on the position, pace and depth of your opponent's shot — and you have only one chance to get it right.

You are in charge of your serve, and you can take your time. You can place the ball where you want it — just decide what part of the court you want to aim at. You decide, too, what spin to put on the ball, if any. You choose how hard you hit it. Then, on top of all this, if you foul up the first time, you get another go!

With so much in your favour, it's positively criminal not to take full advantage. A good player MUST develop a good serve.

You're probably wondering, 'What about the third point about the serve?' It is the most important of all. It's all about what you do with your free hand. On the serve, what you do with your 'free' hand is very bit as important as what you do with the racket hand.

The whole stroke depends on how you place the ball in the air before you hit it. 'Place' is the operative word. It conveys far more precisely the care and accuracy you need than the more commonly used words such as 'toss' or 'throw-up'. Placing the ball in the right position is the critical factor in the service. I would say that as much as 90% of service faults are down to bad ball-placement — it's too low (most common!), too high, too far forward, too far back, too far to one side.

To be consistently good at serving, your placement of the ball must be inch-perfect — every time. That's why, even with so many things in your favour, the service is still a tough shot to master. I said 'in theory it should be the easiest shot' — however, reality doesn't always match up to theory.

Just watch the top players at Wimbledon. These guys hit thousands of serves. You'd think that surely, they'd never miss one — but they do. They are happy — in fact, delighted — if they achieve a 70% success rate on their first serve.

ven the very best servers rarely complete a match without at
east one double-fault.

So, no matter what your general standard is, the thing to
work on is placement — toss, throw-up — whatever you
want to call it. Get it right, and the rest of the stroke is easy
– well comparatively easy.

The technique

The action of the stroke is just like that of throwing a ball —
or even a javelin. Give Fatima Whitbread a tennis racket and
she would have a great serve — provided she could get the
ball placement right.

It's this co-ordination of placing the ball in the air and
throwing the racket-head, that the service is all about.

Just as with groundstrokes, I wouldn't worry too much
about the style. The only really important factors are putting
the ball in the right place and getting the racket into a
'throwing' position.

Look on the 'throwing' position as a 'back-scratcher'. You
have to get the racket-head into a position where you can
scratch your back with it — how you get it there is
immaterial. Everyone develops their own style.

It is possible to hit a perfectly good serve by starting off
with the racket already in the throwing position. I've seen
world-class players resort to this when they have temporarily
lost their rhythm in the full swing. However, the best servers
have a long, fluent swing, which builds up towards an
explosive climax at contact with the ball.

'Explosive' is another word which I use deliberately. A good
serve is like a shot from a gun — you take your time lining up
the barrel, then you take aim and FIRE.

Take a look at Boris Becker serving. You can see him lining
himself up, just like a cannon being aimed. He lines up his
feet, sets his sights, points his racket — and then belts the
ball as hard as he can.

Boris Becker's massive serve is the foundation of his whole
game. He knows he's not going to lose his serve unless
something goes badly wrong, so he is able to cast all caution
aside when his opponent is serving and go for broke on his
returns. Conversely, if Boris loses confidence in his own
serve, the rest of his game can disintegrate. Even a player
with what is possibly the best serve in the world, still has to
practise and practise, just to make sure that his placement of
the ball is consistently accurate.

Let's just go through the mechanics of the swing. I don't like to be dogmatic about anything — after all, there are always players who succeed by breaking all the so-called rules. In the case of the serve, John McEnroe is the obvious example. His action defies logic, but his serve is one of the best ever. That's not to say, however, that I would recommend the sideways-on stance which McEnroe adopts. Its effectiveness is the exception which proves the rule.

The Becker-style line-up is much more practical for the average player. He has his feet set comfortably about 12-18 inches apart, lined up so that his left shoulder (as a right-handed player) points towards his target.

It is from this position that you start the swing. You should have your hands almost together, the left hand which holds the ball, just resting against the racket-handle. As you start the take-back, the arms move in tandem — the racket-arm swings straight back and the ball-arm swings forward in direct line with the target. As you start the swing, rock back, putting all your weight on to the back foot.

The best grip for the service is the continental or chopper grip. Note the weight on the front foot at the ready position before it rocks back as the swing starts.

Left is the Becker 'gun' position, beautifully lined up. See the contrast with McEnroe's line-up, above, with his back almost facing the net. McEnroe has to pivot on the ball of his right foot to get into the hitting position.

41

The service swing. Most players prefer to hold only one ball.

Keeping your elbow high, bring the racket round into the 'back-scratching' position, the wrist cocked ready for the throwing action. If you've got your timing right, you will reach the throwing position just as your left arm sweeps up into a vertical position and releases the ball.

Then, literally, you throw the racket-head up and forward to meet the ball at the highest point of your swing, so that you are hitting down on the ball. As you start the throwing action, transfer your weight on to the front foot, so your right leg swings right through.

The racket-head should follow through on the line of the ball, finishing, on a basic flat serve, past your left side.

Just as with the groundstrokes, it is crucial to get your body-weight going forward in the direction of the shot to produce power.

Don't underestimate the importance of a good leg-action. Becker once again makes an ideal example. He has a tremendous knee-bending action, enabling him to spring up with his full body-weight behind the ball.

A great serve is a combination of a rhythmic swing and a good leg-action — this way you can achieve maximum racket-head speed in the hitting-zone. Having said this, the best action in the world is useless if you can't put the ball in the right place — this single aspect is absolutely critical.

42

The importance of the toss is becoming more and more evident these days — it has even influenced the design of tennis clothing. Most players like to hold only one ball as they serve, so they have a pocket or clip for the spare ball. The development of modern rackets has also magnified the importance of ball positioning — they can be swung so much faster, being lighter and stronger, and so there is less margin for error in the throw-up.

Even the very best players feel they can only place the ball accurately with consistency if they have only one ball in their hand. That way the ball can rest lightly in the fingers, ready for release as the arm comes up.

The 'feel' of what the top players do is literally that of 'putting' the ball in the air. It is not a throw or a toss — it is a placement.

Ideally, you should put the ball at exactly the right height for the centre of the racket-head to make contact at the very highest point of the swing — when the racket-arm is straight. At the moment of impact, the ball should be almost 'hanging' in the air, stationary — at the top of its rise, before it starts to fall.

That's a tough objective to achieve — the timing has to be perfect. So, for most people it's better to throw the ball a little higher than what would otherwise be ideal.

Ivan Lendl used to have a very high toss, making contact as much as a foot below the highest point. These days he has adjusted his toss by about nine inches — and in doing so has evolved a more consistent serve.

Players such as Roscoe Tanner and Kevin Curren, both explosive servers, actually hit the ball while it is still going up. This fits in with their fast, short actions which have a restricted take-back. The method is unorthodox, but it's effective. To serve like that, you have to be very strong in the arm and wrist.

Keep the left hand pointing up at the ball as the racket reaches the 'back-scratcher' position.

Putting technique into action

To check the correct height at which you personally need to place the ball, stand on tip-toe and reach up with your racket as far as you can go. The centre point of the strings is where you want to make contact with the ball — so that's the height to which you need to throw it.

Remember, though, that if you are going to jump into the serve — and most of the great servers today have both feet off the ground when they hit the ball — you will need to add on a few extra inches to your placement of the ball.

It is clearly important to make maximum use of every inch. Even the simplest diagram will show that hitting the ball over the net and down into the service box allows very little margin for error, even for very tall players. Also, the harder you hit the ball, the less margin for error you have — every inch you can gain by stretching or jumping is an advantage.

Therefore, you must never hit the serve with a bent arm — this is simply sacrificing crucial height and power. To help you to stretch up to the ball, keep your left arm up, reaching for the sky after you've released the ball.

The height of the ball is not the only important factor — the position is just as vital. On a basic, flat serve, the ball should be placed so that it would land about nine to twelve inches inside the baseline.

If you can imagine a clock-face immediately in front of the server, the ball would be positioned at the 'midday' position for a flat serve, at 'five past' for a sliced serve, and at 'five to' for a kick serve. Having said that, today's great servers can hit all three service variations with the same toss — but that requires tremendous wrist strength and flexibility.

Great servers develop that ability to prevent the receiver from reading the direction of the serve from the angle of the toss — but that is an advanced technique and skill which you should only work on once you have completely mastered the basic action.

An average club-standard player should aim to place the ball about nine inches to the right for the slice serve, and about the same distance to the left for a kick serve. The more advanced your standard of play, the further forward you can afford to place the ball. Club players still need to position the ball about nine inches inside the baseline, while a top server such as Becker or Pat Cash will place the ball so that it would fall nearer two feet inside the court — this helps carry them in to the net behind the serve.

Practise placement by laying a ball box or a book on the court where you want the ball to land. Then go through the motions of the service, releasing the ball and letting it drop instead of hitting it. Work on that action to place the ball up — so you can get it to land on target consistently.

If you find you are not getting real power in your racket-throwing action, try this exercise. Get an old racket which you no longer use, and find a wide open space. Then, just throw the racket as hard as you can — you could use the back netting of a court to save yourself from having to keep fetching it.

Getting a grip

Just as with the basic groundstrokes, it's important to ensure that you keep a nice, relaxed grip on the racket. Don't be tempted to grip too hard — you need a loose grip so that your wrist is flexible enough to whip the racket over the ball.

The grip you need is normally the 'shake hands' or 'chopper' grip. Some players do use a backhand grip for serving, but there is less room for variation on the grip than with groundstrokes.

In normal circumstances, the first service would be hit flat, with as much power as you can muster. The racket-head meets the ball square on, imparting little or no spin, but rather relying on power and direction to put the receiver under pressure.

The second serve requires a built-in margin for error — and this you achieve by using either slice or top spin, as in the kick serve. Both serves can be effective, depending on the court surface and the receiver's strengths and weaknesses. If you are a right-hander playing a right-hander, then the kick serve lets you keep the ball on his backhand side. Or, if you are a right-hander serving to a left-hander, then the natural swing and movement of the sliced serve will still take the ball on to the backhand side.

The kick serve

You hit the kick serve by throwing the ball to the left (if you are right-handed), and hitting up and over the ball — just the same as hitting a top-spin groundstroke. The top spin will allow you to serve at least two feet over the net and still get the ball down into the service box.

If you hit the kick serve correctly, the follow-through will take the racket down past your right leg — not the left side as in the slice and flat serves.

The sliced serve

If you throw the ball up to the right, you can curl the racket round the side of the ball, imparting side spin which gives you extra control — in other words, a sliced serve.

Obviously, the ideal is not to have to hit a second serve at all — the art is to get a high percentage of first serves in..

First serve nerves

If you are missing a lot of first serves, try taking some pace off. Sometimes it is better to hit a ball at three-quarters pace and get a first serve in, than to have to hit a second serve, particularly on a big point.

Nerves — what we call 'elbow' — can have a disastrous effect on the serve. Generally speaking, what happens is that

For the kick serve, throw the racket-head up so that it brushes the back of the ball, imparting the top-spin. Note how the follow through comes down past the right hip on the kick serve.

you make a low toss, then end up dumping the ball into the net. Miroslav Mercir, ranked in the world top five used to resort to serving underarm at the start of his career, so badly was he affected by 'elbow'.

Take it easy. If you feel your toss is too low or is wrongly placed, don't try to hit the ball. You can always abandon the serve without it being called as a fault — just as long as you don't swing the racket at the ball.

If your ball-placement has gone wrong, just let the ball drop, compose yourself and start again. Force yourself to throw the ball up higher — if necessary, exaggerate. Break the tension in your arm and try to 'feel' yourself releasing the ball correctly.

Remember, you are in charge of the service — you call the shots. The serve is your chance to dominate the point, so make the most of that opportunity.

The smash

Get yourself a good service — and you'll automatically develop a good smash too. The principles are exactly the same, and the smash is just like a serve — except your opponent has placed the ball in the air for you to hit.

What matters here is good footwork. You must move well to get underneath the ball. As soon as you spot the lob going up, back-pedal to get underneath the ball as it drops. Turn yourself to stand sideways on to the ball, just as you line yourself up to serve, and throw your racket at the ball in the same way.

The action is similar to that of the serve, even down to the 'back-scratch' position, which you need to get into good and early. As you position yourself under the dropping ball, point your left hand up towards it. This will help you to judge the height at which you should make contact. Just as with serving, make sure you hit the ball with a straight arm — if you try to smash with a bent arm, you lose all your power.

The most effective smashers jump to gain extra height and to really hit down on the ball. This also gives the advantage of putting the body's full weight behind the shot.

The smash is a very satisfying shot, allowing you to be as aggressive as you like. You've got more scope than on the serve, since you have the whole court to aim at, so enjoy belting the ball as hard as you can.

Of course, you don't have to thrash the cover off the ball — some of the most effective smashes are best described as angled placements, hit with controlled pace, using the wrist to direct the ball.

Whatever sort of smash you hit, be dominant. The fact that your opponent has lobbed the ball into the air means that you have him on the run. So — don't hand back the initiative by being tentative and half-hearted with your smash — really go for it!

You may be faced with two types of lob to play back — the attacking top-spin lob and the defensive sky-scraper. If you receive a top-spin lob, you must hit it in the air. Once you let it bounce, you've had it. You must make a move early and fast to get under the ball as it arrives on your side of the net.

On the other hand, if you are facing a high, defensive lob, which is dropping almost vertically, you may not be able to hit it on the full. Instead, get back behind the ball and let it

The key point on the smash is to position yourself underneath the dropping ball so that you can make contact in front as the racket is on the way down. Point the left hand at the ball to help judge the height, and make sure the racket arm is at full stretch on contact.

bounce before smashing it. A very high lob will bounce high enough for you to hit it just like a serve. If you think it will not bounce that high, then it is probably safer to take it on the full. The knack is to judge carefully and assess each situation quickly.

Make up your mind early and be aggressive. Get the racket up into the throwing position early and stretch up to meet the ball as high as possible. Hit with a good, long follow-through, so you can really punish those lobs!

CHAPTER SEVEN

Tactical shots

These are the shots you can rely on when you are, perhaps, under pressure, or you find your opponent — or yourself, out of position. They are the strokes which give you the use of the whole court to fox your opponent.

The lob

When I was younger, I used to regard the lob as a shot for sissies — one used by players who were too weak or cowardly to go for a passing shot. I suppose my only excuse was lack of experience!

Nowadays I see the lob as one of the most essential strokes in a player's repertoire. That's because, in the modern game, the lob has become much more of an attacking stroke. The increasing use of top-spin, combined with the lighter structure of rackets, allows the lob to be a very aggressive shot which can be used to great effect.

There are two kinds of lob — the attacking lob, hit with top-spin, and the defensive lob, which is hit flat or with back-spin.

When you hit a lob with top-spin, you can hit it fast and with a lower trajectory. You can aim it just over the net-player's reach, and let the top-spin drag the ball down inside the court.

The defensive lob is more of a sky-scraper, and you need to hit it very high and to the back of the court. When you hit such a shot, your objective is not only to get the ball over the net-player, but also to give yourself time to get back into position.

But don't let that give you the idea that you should only hit a lob when your opponent is at the net. Far from it. The lob is very effective at breaking up a baseline rally — it does it by disrupting your opponent's rhythm.

Of course, when you are forced out of court by an angled drive, the best response you can give is a lob, or semi-lob, deep to the baseline which gives you time to return to the centre of the court.

The lob is a really important tactical shot — but it is probably still under-used by most players who, perhaps just as I did, see it as a sign of weakness.

Lobbing in practice

The good news about the top-spin lob is that you can hit it two different ways — the bad news is that I can't teach you one of them!

The easy method is just a variation of the basic top-spin forehand drive. You just deepen the loop in the backswing to come underneath the ball a little more. You hit up on the ball, rolling your wrist over on impact to give it top-spin. The follow-through carries the racket up for a very high finish.

The action is more of a brushing on the back of the ball than the very firm contact you have to make for the drive.

To help the element of disguise which makes the top-spin lob so effective, you make the same preparation and backswing as for the drive. As you start the forward swing, drop your wrist to bring the racket-head low, so that it comes up to meet the ball from below.

You should transfer your body-weight forward as you step into the shot. In all respects it is like the forehand drive — but with a higher trajectory.

The second method of hitting a top-spin lob is something I can only describe to you — it can't be taught, it's a knack.

What it is is a whipped shot. It's all wrist. It's more or less the same action as the one I have described — but you do it twice as fast. The racket travels very fast from underneath to above the ball.

This option of shot is only open to players with a very wristy style. Instead of rolling the wrist over the ball, you flick it. It is like a table-tennis shot and requires very fast hands and a strong wrist. There is virtually no margin for error because the racket travels so fast, but if you strike it well, the shot has no reply. The ball whips up and over the net-player before he has the chance to go back.

This shot is the ultimate attacking lob — a very modern shot which requires perfect timing, but is wonderfully effective when executed well. The ball carries so much top spin that, even if it doesn't clear the net-player, the dipping flight can make it very tough to smash.

The defensive lob is a much more basic, simple shot — one to play only when you are under pressure from a net attack. Generally players hit this shot with some under spin for control and with a lot of height to carry it to the back of the court.

Just as with the attacking shot, it is an adaptation of the

basic drive, for both forehand and backhand. Line up for the shot just as for the groundstroke, but open the racket-face before contact to slice underneath the ball. Then, hit up on the ball, lengthening the follow-through to finish high.

The higher you hit the ball, the more time you win yourself to regain position. The effect of the back spin will be to hold the ball in the air, so that when it starts to fall, it will drop almost vertically.

Although it is a defensive shot, often played at full stretch, the stroke requires a good touch. Try to 'feel' the ball into the air — get the feeling of 'lifting' the ball up. Even under severe pressure, try to get your body-weight behind the shot — or it will fall too short. The more back spin you can put on the ball, the harder you can afford to hit the shot, as the spin holds the ball in the air.

The drop shot

Top-level players today are so fit that the drop-shot has almost become obsolete in professional tennis — certainly among the men, except occasionally on clay courts. But it's still a useful shot for top women and club players to master.

Disguise is fundamental to the shot's success. As you prepare to play a drop shot, you must convince your opponent that you are shaping up to play an attacking sliced approach. Then, instead of hitting firmly through the ball, at the last second you open the racket-face and come right underneath the ball, lifting it gently over the net with back spin. The best drop-shot will land on the court with the impact of a poached egg!

Today, at top level, the drop-shot is played almost exclusively on the backhand side. This is because very few players in the modern game ever hit a sliced forehand, so it is very difficult for them to disguise a drop-shot played on that side. On the other hand, most players can hit a sliced backhand, and therefore they can play a drop-shot from that side without any change in their normal preparation.

You need a high take-back and, as the racket comes down to meet the ball, your hand turns the racket-face to come through under the ball. A lot of players make the mistake of not following through with the racket, but they must, just as for the basic drive.

The drop is a touch shot, which you need to 'feel' with your hands. Slicing the racket-head under the ball floats it up

Drop the racket-head for the lob so that you can hit right up and through the ball. Get the bodyweight behind the shot and follow through long and high.

The key to hitting the drop shot is to open the racket-face and bring it through right underneath the ball, floating it up with back-spin for a soft landing.

in the air — you need enough height on the ball to carry it over the net, while the back spin holds the ball in the air and gives it a soft landing.

Play a drop-shot when you have manoeuvred your opponent out of the court, forcing a short return. Step in as if you are going to slide an approach, then slice the racket under the ball and aim for the far side of the court, from where your opponent has just come. If your drop-shot is short enough, your opponent will have to run the full diagonal length of the court to reach it.

Once you've played the shot, move in behind it to mid-court, so that you cannot be caught out by a drop-shot reply.

It is very risky to play a drop-shot from behind your own baseline. Firstly, it's a tougher shot to judge accurately, and secondly, it gives your opponent more time to reach it. In fact, try not to overdo the drop-shot — keep it as a surprise tactic. The more you play the shot, the more easily your opponent will read it — and he'll get the impression that you are not confident of winning the point any other way.

Chris Evert is probably the best drop-shotter in the game. Because she hits her basic forehand with just a suspicion of slice, she can produce a drop-shot off the forehand with ease and great deception. Even so, she only uses the shot once, perhaps twice in a match — and then always when she is leading in a game.

She knows, and you should remember too, that the drop is a risky shot, especially if you are trying to save a big point. Use it to put the nail in the coffin, but don't try to use it to stay alive.

The half-volley

The best advice I can give you about the half-volley is, quite simply, 'Don't ever play the shot'. As far as I'm concerned, the shot is a real 'no-no', only to be used if you absolutely can't avoid it.

For starters, never hit a half-volley when you can step further in and volley the ball. Then, never hit a half-volley when you can hold back, let the ball bounce, then attack it off the ground.

The very nature of the half-volley makes it a tough shot to control. You are meeting the ball as it bounces — and the chances are you will be in a half-court position. This means you have to get the ball up and over the net — low enough to stay in the court. Furthermore, it is a defensive shot, so never play it by choice, only when you have to.

Basically, it's a blocked shot. You don't swing at the ball. Instead, you close the racket-face and just meet the ball in front as it bounces, blocking it back over the net. To do this, you need a full knee-bend so that you can get right down to meet the ball on the bounce and keep the racket-head above the wrist.

If you are caught at your feet and have to hit a half-volley, don't go for a winner. Try to get depth on the shot and try for length rather than pace. Play the shot down the middle of the court to avoid opening up an angle for a passing shot. You have to be flexible. Bend at the waist and knees and hit the ball with a brushing action, following through along the line of the shot.

This is a shot which is easier to make with the big-head 'maxi' rackets because the 'sweet spot', which generates greater pace under control, is much larger. The best exponents of the half-volley tend to be those who use 'maxi' rackets, such as Paul Annacone and Pam Shriver, who have a natural flair for the shot. Even so, I'm sure they were told the same thing as youngsters, 'Don't use a half-volley unless you have to'.

The backhand smash

If I had my way, there would be no such thing as a backhand smash — I simply don't recognise any need to play the shot, and don't recall ever having played a single backhand smash in my life. I say this because every player should be quick-footed and flexible enough to adapt the basic forehand smash for a lob over their backhand side.

The fact remains, though, that some players will always be more comfortable hitting a backhand smash than trying to perform contortions to take the ball on the forehand.

In that case, as soon as the ball is hoisted over your left shoulder, pivot around to the left, taking the racket back with your elbow high and the racket-head pointing to the ground. As you prepare for the shot, your back should be facing the net.

Sweep the racket arm up and forward, snapping the wrist forward to gain racket-head speed. Aim to meet the ball in front of you and make contact with the arm straight. Your follow-through should take the racket-head down past your right hip (right-handed players).

Hitting an outright winner from a backhand smash is almost impossible unless you have unbelievable strength in the wrist and arm — so aim for depth and control rather than outright power. Best of all, don't even think about playing the shot!

CHAPTER EIGHT

Tactics and strategy

The first thing you have to understand about tennis is that there is no such thing as standard 'right tactics'. What may be a winning strategy against one person may play right into the hands of another opponent of similar overall standard.

The essence of tactical play is analysing your opponent's game to discover what type of shots he likes to play and which he doesn't enjoy — and tailoring your game accordingly. The art is to make your opponent play the kind of shots he doesn't want to hit.

However, it's not quite as simple as that. Suppose your opponent has a weak backhand. The obvious tactic would seem to be to hit as many balls as possible on to that weakness. But what if your best shot is the cross-court forehand which takes the ball to your opponent's forehand? You might not be as effective hitting your forehand into the backhand corner.

You have to discover whether you are more effective playing to your strength, rather than to your opponent's weakness. In general, unless you know your opponent's game well, always start a match by playing to your own strengths — even if by doing so you ignore the opposition's weaknesses.

If you start to lose, adapt your tactics. There's never anything wrong in playing to your strengths. Indeed, if you do this, you give yourself time to assess your opponent. Don't be panicked into changing your game after just a few points.

Remember, on his side, your opponent wants you to hit the kind of shots you don't enjoy playing — so don't give him that privilege unless you can't avoid it. Your tactics must depend on the player you are facing — but first and foremost you should aim to impose your game on him.

Tactics in match play

If you are a natural serve/volley player, it's likely that you are less confident and not as steady from the back of the court. If you are up against a strong groundstroker, you are unlikely to be able to outrally them from the back — therefore you must try to win by attacking with your natural game.

Also, if you are a serve/volleyer, don't be put off if you are passed a few times early on. The more times you attack the net, the harder it will be for your opponent to keep passing you.

Lew Hoad, Wimbledon Champion in 1956/57, once told me he always felt confident he could win on clay courts by serve/volleying. He believed that no player in the world at that time could keep passing him for three sets! They might do it for two sets — but by then he could read the direction of the passing shot like a book, and so could start making the volleys.

The same applies in reverse. If you are a natural baseliner with good groundshots, don't assume that you have to go into the net when you get on a fast court.

Of course it's sensible to go in when you have an opening — but be patient — work for that opening. Don't just charge in because you think it's the thing to do on a fast court.

Bjorn Borg proved that Wimbledon can be won from the baseline — on the other hand, I believe that Ivan Lendl has failed at Wimbledon in the past because he has tried to do something he's not really good at — serve/volleying.

I'm sure Lendl could have enjoyed better success at Wimbledon if he played to his strengths from the back of the court, coming in to the net only when he had a relatively easy volley to make.

Similarly, Boris Becker will never win in Paris on the clay courts by trying to play from the back like Lendl or Mats Wilander — but he could win in Paris by playing his own attacking game.

Winning tennis is all about playing to your strengths while being adaptable and flexible enough to change your tactics when it's obvious you need to. Above all, you must be positive. Never think about missing a shot. Instead, think in front, like a chess master.

The attacking advantage

As soon as you sense you are putting your opponent under pressure, take up a more aggressive position — you should do this automatically.

If you hit a hard drive, deep into the corner, step in a yard or two in anticipation of the short ball. Never let the ball drop too low — move forward to take it close to the top of the bounce. One of the most common mistakes in the whole

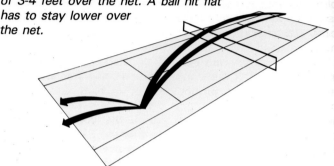

Compare the flight-path of the flat ground shot and the top-spin stroke. When you are playing from the back of the court, hitting with top spin allows a safety margin of 3-4 feet over the net. A ball hit flat has to stay lower over the net.

game is waiting too long for the ball to arrive, instead of going to meet it.

Always try to anticipate what shot your opponent is about to play. Watch how he lines up for the shot, the way his shoulders turn, whether his wrist drops to indicate a top-spin shot. The earlier you can figure the type of shot you are facing, and the pace and length of the ball, the easier it is to prepare for your reply.

Singles tactics

Your aim, when playing singles, is to dominate your opponent, imposing your game on him so that he doesn't play on your own weaknesses.

How you do that depends on the type of game you play and what your strengths are. If you are a serve/volleyer, then put pressure on by getting as many first serves in as possible, and by closing in quickly on the net.

The technique of following your serve into the net depends on being able to get in fast. That demands a service action which allows you to be stepping into the court as you finish your service swing.

Follow the direction of the serve as you go in to the net. For example, if you serve down the middle of the court, you must follow in down the centre of the court. If, on the other hand, you serve wide to the angle, you must follow in the same way. By serving wide you open up the angle for the

58

turn down the line — so you must make sure you have that side covered.

When you come in behind your serve, you must get inside the service line by at least a foot or two to play your first volley, so your first steps behind the serve should be very fast, taking you deep into the court. When you reach mid-court, you can be slowing down, so that you are stationary and composed when you play the volley.

From here, after you've played the first volley, you should aim to close in on the net still further. If your first volley is really deep, pinning your opponent to the back fence, get in so close that your nose is over the net! The closer you get to the net, the better you can punch the ball away from above net height. Also, if you are close, it is harder for your opponent to dip the ball, forcing you to volley up. So swarm all over him! His only reply is likely to be a defensive lob — which you have plenty of time to go back and smash.

If, however, your volley is not really deep enough, back off a little to give yourself time to read the direction of the passing shot. But you still want to keep the pressure on your opponent — so don't retreat too far. Force him to go for the pass.

If you find you are caught behind the service box when you follow your serve in, you can assume that your first strides have been too slow or that your service toss was too far back to let your weight swing through, so carrying you into the court.

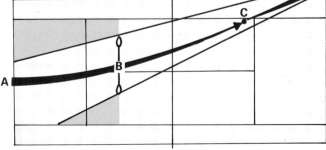

The effect of a wide-angled service. The server, A, follows the line of the serve to B. The diagram shows how much of the court he can cover without difficulty. The shaded areas show the only target areas for the receiver. His only realistic shot is down the line, where he has twice as much court to aim at.

Serving sense

When you serve from the right-hand court, roughly 70%
should be directed down the middle (presuming you are
playing a right-hander). When you serve from the left-hand
court, the break-down should be more in the region of 80%
wide to the backhand and 20% down the centre.

Even if a player is stronger on the backhand, you shouldn'
serve too much to the forehand. The forehand swing can
generate much greater pace on the ball than the backhand,
and even players with great backhands find it tough to pass
good volleyer when they are forced out wide to return the
service.

Tactics in play

If you are an attacking player, but constantly find yourself
caught at your feet by the return of serve, hold back and
come in on the second ball. If your opponent has got into the
groove of hitting half-court returns, by staying back you will
have a short ball to deal with and you can attack the net
behind a sliced approach.

The same principle applies to going in to the net as does
with following in your serve. Follow the line of the ball — so
if you play your approach shot into the backhand corner, you

*The centre theory. The server aims down the centre
line and follows in to position B. The receiver does not
have much of an angle to play the passing shot. The
closer the volleyer gets to the net, the easier it is to
reach the passing shot.*

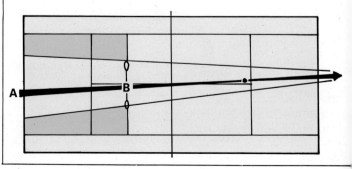

must follow it in to a position about two-thirds across the court, in order to cover the likely passing shot down the line. Similarly, if you hit your approach shot down the centre of the court, chase it down the middle.

If you play most comfortably as a baseliner, happier at the back of the court, you must aim to keep your opponent away from the net. Do this by keeping a good length on your groundstrokes. If you can play to his weaknesses without detracting from your own strengths, so much better. Every player has one shot which he favours more than the other, so try to make him play the one he likes least.

Sometimes, the only way to get at a player's weakness is to play deliberately to his strength. It may sound stupid, but it's really very easy to illustrate.

Players who have one big shot — generally the forehand — stand so far across the court that it can be very hard to play the ball to their weaker side. On clay and hard courts Borg, for example, stood 75% across to the backhand side, so that he could take as many balls as possible on the forehand. Andre Agassi positively camps out in his backhand corner. The only way to get on to the weaker backhand is to play the ball wide into their forehand corner to open the court up.

If you are a baseliner, never lose touch with what your opponent is doing. Even though you must never take your eyes off the ball, you must also keep an eye on where he is so that you are not taken by surprise by a sudden net attack.

When you play a baseline rally, you can play the ball four or five feet over the net to enable you to get enough depth of shot to put your opponent under pressure. If he is at the net, your shot must be a low one, preferably hit with top spin, to try to catch him at his feet.

What if your opponent is a volleyer? Firstly, don't make the mistake of trying to hit a passing shot off the first ball. Concentrate on keeping the ball low, forcing him to volley up. If you are under pressure and can't make the passing shot, hoist up a lob to get yourself some time to recover.

It's worth remembering that some players, particularly tall people with long arms, volley much better when they are stretching for the ball. They like you to go for the space because they have the reach to cover it. They are often less confident when they have to deal with a ball which is hit straight at them.

Similarly, some players love to volley a fast return and find it much harder to play a shot which has little pace. It can be much harder to generate your own speed on the ball if your opponent doesn't give you enough pace to use. This applies as well to ground shots as it does to volleys. Some players love to play against hard-hitters — they can just block the ball, without needing to swing too hard, taking the pace from the shot they receive. Types like these are even less happy when confronted by a slow ball which has no speed to assist its return. It's all part of the ploy to make your opponent play the shot he doesn't enjoy.

If, for example, you are playing someone who hits with heavy top spin, use heavily sliced groundshots which keep very low — it's tough to hit top-spin shots off a very low ball. Or, if you are facing a double-handed backhand, hit short,

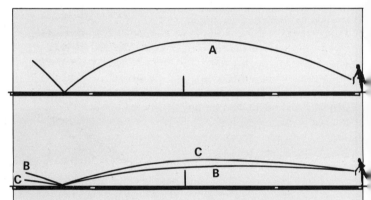

You can see the different uses of the various types of ground stroke. The top-spin shot, A, can be hit with 4 feet of clearance over the net and still land in court. The top-spin will make the ball bounce high, forcing the baseliner to play the return shoulder- or even head-high, which is very tiring and can be hard to control.
The flat drive, B, has a regular trajectory and an even bounce. The height of the shot over the net is governed by the speed of the shot. Hit very hard, a groundstroke with no controlling spin needs to be aimed low over the net to land in court. The slower the shot the higher it can be played over the net. The sliced return will tend to float in the air as the back-spin holds it up. The bounce on a sliced shot depends on the court surface. On a fast court such as grass, a sliced ball will shoot through low and is ideal as an approach shot. On some hard courts, a sliced shot will tend to 'stop' on landing, making the return difficult to judge.

wide-angled balls which force them to bend and stretch. An opponent who is not very tall will have difficulty with 'moon-ball' shots — high, looping groundshots which will have him struggling to play shoulder- or head-high returns behind the baseline.

When two players are basically the same, the winner will be the one who can vary his game and change the pace, introducing the unexpected, without detracting from his own strengths.

It is easy to show how little margin for error there is on the flat serve. In figure B, below, only a server of at least 6ft tall can hit a serve in a straight line and land it inside the service court. That is using his full height, and with racket arm fully extended. It is obvious that no player can afford to sacrifice height by serving with a bent arm or by not using their full height. For every player the second serve must be hit with spin to provide a safety margin.

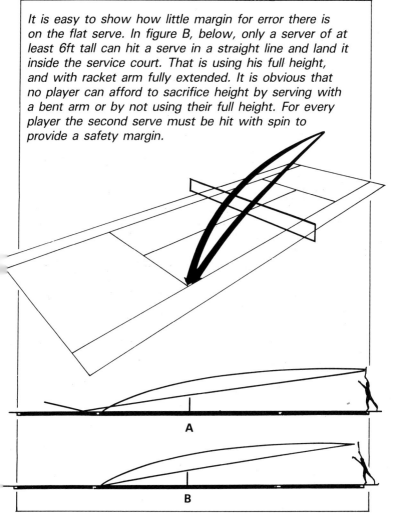

A

B

Working the opening for the drop shop. Use the drop shot sparingly when you have engineered the opening. The ideal time is when you have played a deep drive angled into the corner, forcing your opponent out of court and behind the baseline. If the return is to the half court, you have your chance. Step in and float your drop shot across the court, lifting it over the net with back-spin. Your opponent has to run almost the full diagonal length of the court to reach it. Follow your drop shot in, just in case you are playing against Speedy-Gonzales. You should be able to cut off any retrieving shot he can make.

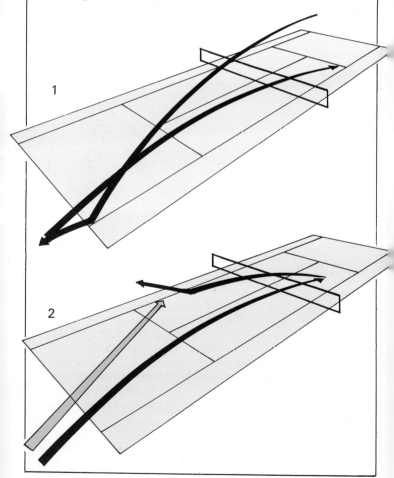

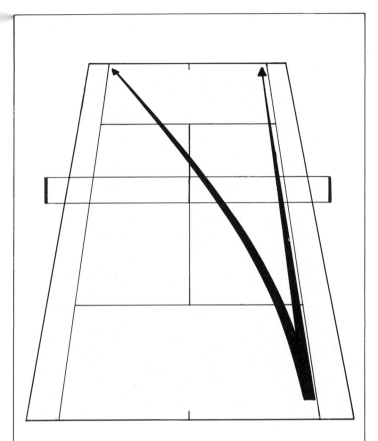

If you are struggling with your timing and missing a lot
of shots, concentrate on playing the ball over the
centre of the net where it is lowest. Try to play your
shots across the court, from corner to corner. This has
two benefits. You are hitting over the lowest part of
the net and you have the longest distance in which to
get the ball down into court. You can therefore afford
to give the ball more height and pace, and still land it
in court. You can afford to hit cross-court shots harder
than those down the line. Hitting down the line you are
going over the high part of the net. You really need to
hit with top-spin to bring the ball down if you are
hitting very hard.

Compare the different trajectories of the top-spin lob and the 'skyscraper'. The top-spin lob is an attacking shot, hit with a relatively low arc, just over the opponent's racket at full stretch. Note how the top-spin lob leaps away on bouncing, showing why you must try to return it without letting it land. The defensive lob has a much higher trajectory. The idea is to give yourself time to regain position while the ball is in the air. The back-spin on a defensive lob holds the ball up and allows it to drop steeply into court. That can make it tough to smash 'on the full'. However, the high bounce does permit a smash off the ground.

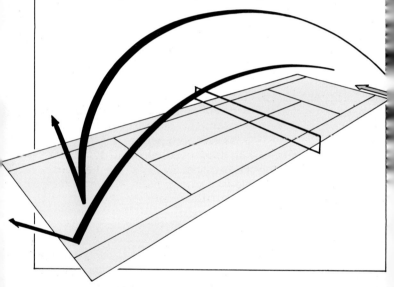

Returning the serve

The return of service is absolutely fundamental to the whole game of tennis — you could argue that it's the most important shot in the game.

It's a shot which depends on the nature of the serve itself. The server dictates what shot the receiver has to play, hence it is a difficult stroke to teach. The pace of modern serves often means that the return has to be something which is an adaptation of the basic groundstroke. There is no time for an orthodox stroke because the ball is coming through too fast.

66

What happens, if your opponent is getting his first serve in, is that you are forced to shorten your backswing so that you 'block' the ball back, using the speed of the serve to generate speed on the return.

How this return goes will depend on whether the server is coming in to the net or not. If he stays back, you can return the ball over the net with a good safety margin, aiming for depth rather than pace. If, on the other hand, he is following the serve in to the net, your return must be low. Don't be tempted to go for a winner on the first ball — often the most effective return is the one aimed at the server's feet, forcing him to play an unwelcome half-volley.

You don't have time, when facing a very fast first serve, to get your feet round into the orthodox position. Instead, you must concentrate on turning your shoulders to allow yourself room to play the stroke. Use a short backswing and punch forward to meet the ball early, blocking it back over the net.

Two of the best service-returners in the modern game take totally different approaches from each other to the job. John McEnroe, at his best, stands well inside the baseline, even against the fastest servers, and takes the ball incredibly early. His return is a flick which, with minimum backswing, lands the ball back at the server's feet with perfect timing.

Jimmy Connors, on the other hand, elects to stand two yards or more behind the baseline. By doing this he gives himself time to take a bigger swing at the ball. Jimmy really attacks his returns, throwing himself into the shot — particularly on the backhand side.

Both of these approaches are successful — you can't say that one is·'the right method'. However, remember that John McEnroe is a genius, and for the average player it is safer to subscribe to the Jimmy Connors approach of giving yourself a bit more time to sight the ball and prepare the shot.

It's a different story if the server misses the first ball. If this happens, as the receiver you should always be looking to punish the second serve. Step in to take it and aim to hit your best shot. Put pressure on the server by 'threatening' on your return. Make him attempt a better second serve than he can necessarily control — under pressure he may be forced into an error.

Just as with groundstrokes, anticipation is vital to the return of serve, especially when the server is strong. You must try to read the direction of the serve. Watch where he places the ball — if it is wide to the right, you can expect a sliced serve. To the left, and you can look for kick serve.

At the very highest level, facing a cannonball server, the

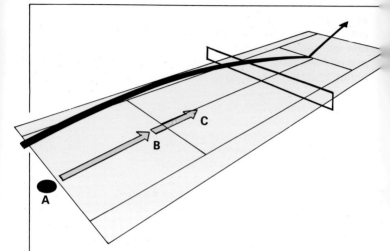

Following the serve in to the net. The first few steps into court must be very fast. From position B, start to slow down so that you are composed and ready to play the first volley from C.

receiver has to make up his mind which way to go before the server strikes the ball.

The fundamental principle of the return of serve is that of getting the ball back into play. The last thing you want to do is give the server cheap points by failing to return the ball — it will only give him added confidence.

Try, instead, to undermine that confidence. If you can keep returning his best serves, even if you don't make winners, you put him under pressure. He'll very possibly react by trying to hit harder and harder, and may lose his rhythm.

If you are missing your returns, try narrowing the court in your mind's eye, then concentrate on returning the ball down the centre. The great Australian, Rod Laver, once told me that if his shots were missing, he didn't take the pace off his returns. Instead he just aimed every shot down the middle, over the lowest part of the net. Then, when he got his eye in better, he could work gradually outwards.

The other thing you can do if you are missing the returns is to stand further back, giving yourself more time. From a deeper position, hit the ball cross court over the lowest part of the net.

Be fully alert as you wait for the serve, well balanced on the balls of your feet and ready to move either way. It is

When you have played the first volley, close in on the net. This puts more pressure on the returner and rushes him into going for a rash shot. Getting in close also makes the volley easier because you can punch it away before the ball has dropped below the net.

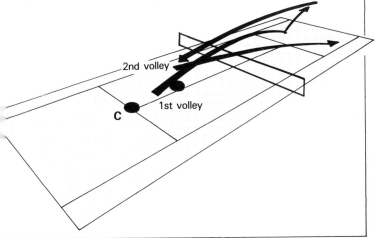

always better to move forward into the return, so that even on a modified groundstroke, your weight goes behind the shot. Be ready to adjust your grip too, according to the shot you play. Wait to receive serve holding the racket in a forehand grip if this is your strongest shot. Always try to take the return on your stronger wing — but if you can't do this, be ready to adapt to the backhand grip. The server will be looking to make you play your weaker shot — so be prepared. Whatever you do, ensure that you get the ball back. Make the server play another shot.

Doubles tactics

The most important thing to remember about playing doubles is that you and your partner are a team. You must work together, knowing what each of you is trying to achieve on each point. Sometimes this understanding takes a long time to establish, but you can help by talking to your partner in between points. You can't tell him exactly what sort of return you are going to try for — that will depend on the serve you have to face — but you can give your partner some help.

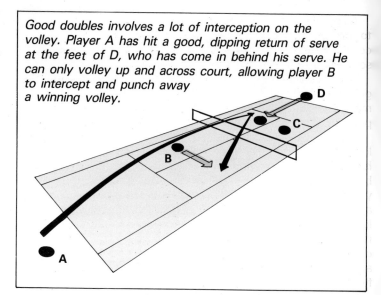

Good doubles involves a lot of interception on the volley. Player A has hit a good, dipping return of serve at the feet of D, who has come in behind his serve. He can only volley up and across court, allowing player B to intercept and punch away a winning volley.

Good doubles play involves trying to engineer openings for your partner to put the ball away, either when you are serving or receiving.

In doubles, it is fundamental to gain control of the net — that means both players being in the forecourt. The doubles game is dominated by the net-players so you should aim to get both players up to the net as early as possible in the rally.

The return of serve is just as vital in doubles as it is in singles — possibly even make so. The percentage return in doubles is cross-court, aimed at the feet of the incoming server — but don't aim too far across court, as this opens up too many angles for the volleyer. The return must be far enough across to make it tough for the server's partner to intercept.

Don't be afraid to smack the odd return down the line to keep the net-player 'honest'. Similarly, you can disrupt the server's rhythm and give yourselves, as receivers, a chance to assume the net position, if you throw up a lob over the net-player.

When serving in doubles, the best players take 15% or so off the pace of the serve to try to ensure that they get the first serve in court. You should direct 80% of these serves to the receiver's backhand — remember always to let your partner know if you are going to vary the direction of the serve by hitting a wide, sliced ball, for example. You must give your partner time to cover his tramline.

Also, when serving, you should aim to follow your serve in to the net, in doubles as in singles, even on the slowest of courts. Bear in mind, there are two of you to cover the court, so it will take a very good return to pass you.

When playing a serve and volley game, don't be tempted to go for a winner on the first volley. Instead, concentrate on making a solid volley, going deep to the baseline, so that you put pressure on the receiver.

If your volley is deep, the response will most probably be a lob. The rule is always to deal yourself with any lob into your half of the court, staying on the offensive whenever possible by smashing it back. If you have to let a lob bounce before you can play it, you lose the initiative in the rally. You should always hold on to an attacking position, so if your partner is lobbed, stay up at the net until you are called back — don't relinquish a net position lightly! If a lob comes down the centre of the court, the partner on the left should take it, assuming he is right-handed, as it will naturally fall on his forehand side.

Good doubles involves a lot of intercepting on the volley, whether by the server's partner going across to cut off the service return, or by the receiver's partner intercepting the server's first volley as he comes in.

To counter a very good cross-court return, top doubles pairs use the tandem formation. The server's partner, C, stands on the same side of the court as the server. He therefore cuts out the cross court return. The server, D, also now has much more room in which to play his first volley. Even if the service return forces a weak volley, player B is likely to have much more ground to cover if he is to intercept.

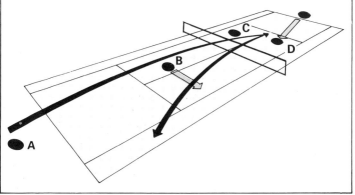

It is also, at top level, a game of bluff and double-bluff. The server's partner may start to move across as if to intercept a cross-court return, thereby inviting a return down his line. But instead of actually going across, he stays, and gets to pick of the return.

'Faking' a move is all part of the game — part of the tactics which make doubles such a fascinating event. It's a thinking game of trying to outwit the opposition — a much more tactical game than singles. In doubles, you are just as important when you are not hitting the ball as when you are playing the shot — your presence and positioning makes all the difference to how your opponents respond.

Generally, the stronger of a doubles pair should play in the left-hand court. This is because he has to play all the most important points — at 15-0, 30-15, 40-30 — where he has to save the situation, and at 0-15, 15-30 and 30-40 when he must try to take advantage of a lead.

Teamwork is the key word. In doubles play, a pair with a good understanding can overcome two individually stronger opponents who don't play as a team.

'Tandem' formation

Tactics are a vital part of the game. Good doubles players are never slow to use the 'tandem' formation to outthink their opponents.

In the 'tandem' system, the server's partner stands at the net on the same side of the court as the server. The aim is twofold — to disrupt a very strong, consistent, cross-court return of serve, or to protect a possible weakness on the volley on the part of the server coming in on one side.

Even if you don't use the tandem formation for one of these specific reasons, it's often a good ploy if you are losing — it can break up your opponents' rhythm.

The essence of doubles

The basic rules of doubles play are to get the first serve in to the backhand, to get in fast to the net — roughly the middle of the service box is best, and to play as a team. Remember, you don't necessarily have to go for a winning shot each time — instead, go for one which will create an opening for you or your partner to make a winner later. Remember — you have someone else to rely on and to set up for those vital winners.

Practice and training

If you watch leading players practising, you'll notice that they don't waste a single ball. Every shot, from start to finish of a practice session, has a purpose in mind.

Both beginners and club players would be well advised to take a leaf out of the pros' book. So many club players, and even good standard ones, practise aimlessly, just knocking the ball back and forth over the net with no real purpose.

A practice plan

Good players are methodical about practice — they work at each shot in turn, getting the 'feel' of the shot, finding a rhythm and working up from a gentle start to full-pace, full-length hitting.

The best way to practise is with a partner of equal standard — or better. Start off by working from the baseline, forehand to forehand, aiming for good length and accuracy of shot.

After about ten minutes of solid hitting, switch to your backhand and drive, backhand to backhand, for a further ten minutes. Then swap to hitting backhand to forehand and vice-versa.

Drills

Once you have worked through all the variations, start on drills. A good one is for one player to hit shots down the lines and for their partner to return every shot cross-court — it means that each player is hitting alternate backhands and forehands and covering a lot of ground in so doing.

If you just stand in one spot to play the ball, tennis could seem an easy game — but in real play, the ball does not return conveniently to where you are standing. Far from it. So the art in tennis is to be able to hit your best shots as you move towards the ball — and that takes practice.

In all practice drills, you should aim to hit at least 20 consecutive shots into the area between the service line and the baseline. One variation in the drill is to play the point out competitively once you've reached the target of 20 shots in the rally.

To vary drills further, try restricting one player to hitting every shot to one side of the court, while his partner can aim to either side. Or try making one player hit every ball with either the forehand or backhand only, so they have to run round the shot if necessary.

Even the most basic of drills can be varied by hitting alternate top-spin and sliced shots, or by hitting a lob on every fifth ball. Restrict one player to the back of the court, while his partner can come in to the net after a certain number of shots.

There are any number of different routines which two players of a similar standard can use. These variations and the imposing of 'conditions' helps to improve your concentration at the same time as working on your strokes.

Rational training

Don't waste court time by practising aimlessly — to hit the ball about without purpose is often worse than not hitting at all, as all it does is breed sloppy habits.

You should concentrate as hard in a practice session as during a match — otherwise boredom sets in and your standard drops.

If you have a weak point, by all means concentrate on getting it right — but not to the exclusion of your strongest shot. Even the best shots need practice to stay 'grooved', so give them a work-out too.

Before you start, spend a few minutes warming up. Run round the court a few times, stretch your hamstrings. Then, when you begin to practise, start hitting gently, but with good depth and control. Build up gradually to full-power hitting.

Once you've warmed up and your shots are 'grooved', put targets down on the court and aim at them. Use a racket cover or a ball can, placed a couple of feet inside the baseline and the same distance from the sideline, then introduce an element of competition by counting the practice hits on target and trying for a better score than your partner.

Targets are a good aid to serving practice as well. Place a target near the centre-line, inside the service box, and another right in the corner. Hit five serves at each one, then serve alternately at the two targets.

Variation is the key-note in practice. It has been proved that it can be counter-productive to spend more than fifteen minutes on one particular shot. Come back to a shot if necessary, but you should always break up the session with something different, so as to keep your mind fresh.

Putting on the pressure

More pressurized practice routines can be achieved by having one player at the net, feeding the practice partner on the baseline. The net-player volleys the return, which allows the groundstroker less time to cover the court between shots.

A two-on-one situation puts even more pressure on the single player. The two players on one side of the net can feed a non-stop supply of balls to keep the singleton on his toes.

Try this drill for overhead shots. Have one player feed the other with a bucket of balls — the net-player must hit the smash, then come forward to touch the net with his racket before going back for the next smash.

Whatever the practice drill, go for accuracy and consistency, rather than sheer power. Getting one return in and the next one out is just a waste of time. Every ball must go in. Once you've grooved in the production of a shot, you can gradually build up the power.

For the last part of a practice session, try to play points (as opposed to playing a normal game format). Use table-tennis type scoring, each player having five service points. The aim is to play each point on its merits, and by playing the points this way, you cut out the psychological implications of what the score is in a real game.

Fitness

Tennis players have to be fit — more so than ever before. The higher the standard of play, the fitter the players need to be.

In the modern game, a lot more thought goes into training. Top players work to develop a blend of strength and mobility, speed and stamina. They need to be strong without becoming muscle-bound, so most of them use weights as part of their training schedules, in conjunction with other exercises, rather than as the main objective.

Training must be keyed to building strength without inhibiting speed, and a circuit of about half a dozen basic exercises with either bar-bells or dumb-bells answers this quite well.

A basic circuit

For tennis players, the most useful exercises are bar-bell curls, step-ups and sit-ups.

For bar-bell curls, stand with your feet apart, holding the bar-bell from underneath, using a weight of no more than 30 lb to begin with. Keep your back straight as you curl your arms upwards, bringing the bar up to your chest, your upper arms tucked in to the body.

For step-ups you need a bench about 18 inches high. Hold a dumb-bell in each hand — again with a total weight of no more than 30 lb — and step on to the bench and back down again with the same foot. Repeat the exercise, with even numbers for each foot.

For sit-ups, lie flat on the ground, your feet anchored under

Barbell curls are a good exercise for building strength in the arms and wrists. Gradually build up the number of repetitions.

a bar (or get a partner to hold them down). Hold the bar-bell across your shoulders, then pull up to a sitting position.

These three exercises strengthen your arms, legs and stomach muscles. The aim is to do a certain number of repetitions of each one, gradually building up the numbers and increasing the weights on the bar-bell. Remember, your main objective is to train agile, flexible muscles, so don't be tempted to overload the weights. They are only there to increase the pressure of the exercise, not to build sheer strength.

There are plenty of routines which do not require weights — press-ups, squat-thrusts, knee-jumps — all of them geared to developing good muscle-tone.

Stamina and speed

A circuit of exercises, both with and without weights, needs to be balanced out by a programme of running — it develops stamina and speed.

Many top players run two or three miles a day, even when they are taking part in a tournament, and between tournaments, when they are working on fitness, they increase the distance to four or five miles a day.

Speed training can most usefully be done on court, where you can simulate game situations. Use the court lines to improvize routines of 'shuttle' runs.

In a basic shuttle run, start at one side line and run to the inside tramline, bending to touch it, then back to the sideline, touching it, then run to the centre service line. Touch this line, then run back to the far inside tramline, touch it, run back to the sideline and finish by running the full width of the court and back.

There are plenty of variations you can use to lengthen the distances. The thing to do is time the first run, and keep trying to improve on that time in all your repetitions.

It is valuable to use the court for sprint training in this way, because in a game of tennis, the maximum distance a player has to run is that of a diagonal line across one end of the court. The game is full of stops, starts and turns, and shuttle runs reproduce that kind of erratic movement.

If you are playing seriously, you should work out a proper training programme with a qualified fitness expert. Every player is an individual, and therefore has different needs when it comes to exercising.

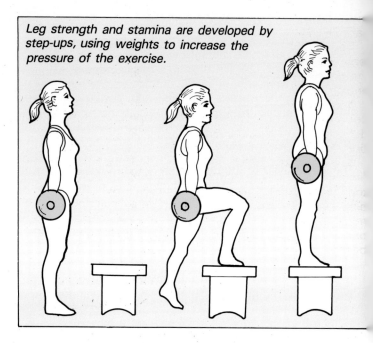

Leg strength and stamina are developed by step-ups, using weights to increase the pressure of the exercise.

Don't just rush headlong into a rigorous training schedule. Never use heavy weights without taking professional advice, or without an expert close at hand to supervize your training. Always warm up properly before you do any explosive type of training — or all you'll achieve will be pulled muscles, or worse.

Overall body-care

Real fitness can only be achieved by following the right kind of diet in conjunction with physical training. Martina Navratilova and Ivan Lendl have personal nutritionists to plan their meals right down to the last calorie. They undergo computer tests to discover their individual metabolism and from there work out exactly what they should eat, how much they should eat, and when they should eat it in order to optimize their performance.

The average club player just needs to be sensible, eating the right kinds of food to produce energy when it is needed and avoiding putting on weight. A balanced diet will include plenty of white meat (chicken and fish) and not too much red meat, plenty of fresh fruit and vegetables and high-carbohydrate foods such as pasta for energy.

You should never play on a full stomach, so plan to eat at least two, if not three hours before you play, and before a match, stock up with plenty of carbohydrates to give you energy.

You'll need plenty of fluids too — take a drink bottle on court to replace lost liquids on change-overs. If you start to dehydrate you'll find you get both physically and mentally tired much more quickly.

In a really long match, the player with the greater physical fitness and sharper concentration will probably come out on top, even against a more talented player — so fitness and preparation are important. They are just as much part of the modern game of tennis as the backhand and forehand. It's all part of what goes to make tennis such a great game — the best.

Islington
Libraries

Index